Informed Consent

poems by

Susan E. Hamilton

Finishing Line Press
Georgetown, Kentucky

Informed Consent

Copyright © 2018 by Susan E Hamilton
ISBN 978-1-63534-504-9 First Edition
All rights reserved under International and Pan-American Copyright Conventions. No part of this book may be reproduced in any manner whatsoever without written permission from the publisher, except in the case of brief quotations embodied in critical articles and reviews.

ACKNOWLEDGMENTS

Only I Get Vertigo ~ *Floating Bridge Review* #4, 2011
After Your 911 Ride ~ *Magnolia News/Queen Anne News* (Feb. 2, 2005), Pacific Publishing Co., Seattle, WA

Publisher: Leah Maines
Editor: Christen Kincaid
Cover Art: Susan E. Hamilton
Author Photo: Eileen H. Bates
Cover Design: Elizabeth Maines McCleavy

Printed in the USA on acid-free paper.
Order online: www.finishinglinepress.com
        also available on amazon.com

        Author inquiries and mail orders:
            Finishing Line Press
             P. O. Box 1626
        Georgetown, Kentucky 40324
               U. S. A.

Table of Contents

Belltown Spleen 1

PATIENT NARRATIVE: I AM SUBJECT 2

He Sent Out Notice to the Rockiest Hills 3

Pre-Op 4

Post-Op 5

Informed Consent 6

Fresh Greyhound 7

Only I Get Vertigo 8

Graphis scripta 9

The Stronger Bond 10

Magrob 11

Travel with me Ormalot, I am cold 12

The Strings 13

Refractory 14

The Sun's Rake 15

After 911 16

Interdigitating Phalanges 17

Power Lines 18

Daphne odora 19

To patients everywhere, and to those who love them and those who tend to their needs.

Belltown Spleen

On her morning commute, head bowed from bus stop to office, the medical writer sidesteps and hop-scotches gelatinous puddles, the beached jellyfish of the other people's expectorant. Beyond the DSHS on 3rd, right on Virginia, past the *Buenos Aires Grill*, adjacent to the *Diamond* parking lot, across 1st Avenue, past the *Real Change* vendor, to Market Tower, the trail of DNA along the way maps an atlas of humanity. She observes a guttural exit from a middle-aged male onto the pavement in front of her. A female runner tosses a wad into bushes mid-stride. A teenager pauses mid-conversation, struts curbside and hurls contempt in a blob as far as he can hock it. Finally, a child, eyes ringed in shadows, yanks a handkerchief from her pocket to catch the mucous, the putrefying egg albumin hanging from her mouth, as she convulses in a paroxysm of coughing.

The medical writer rides the elevator to Floor 7 and her daily job, writing narratives for clinical trial subjects with cystic fibrosis (CF).

Patient Number: 00501
Demographics: age 10, white female
Forced Expiratory Volume in 1 Second: 32% predicted (based on
    healthy 10-year-old girl)
Medical History: malnutrition, failure to thrive, chronic sinusitis, CF
    related diabetes, pancreatic insufficiency, CF end-stage lung
    disease
Serious Adverse Event (SAE): pulmonary exacerbation (lung disorder)
X-ray: bilateral opacities superimposed upon chronic bronchiectasis
Microbiology: sputum culture positive for *Pseudomonas aeruginosa*,
    Burkholderia cepacia, and methicillin-resistant *Staphalococcus
    aurelius*

Status: SAE remains unresolved at the time of data cutoff. Subject
    remains on lung transplant list.

PATIENT NARRATIVE: I AM SUBJECT

There is no horizon.
There is nothing before and after his point in time.
Color provides unnecessary distraction.

Patient number: 00801	Diagnosis: Prostate Cancer	Initial Gleason Score: 4+3

Era	Serious Adverse Events
Early time	fractured left humerus, sutures across patella
Middle time	surgical repair of herniated discs
Metastatic time	black shadows on white; white shadows on black

The ageless white male was screened for the study in 2005 AD. He received his first dose of study drug at birth. In addition to his diagnosis of being alive, he had a history of parents, breaking new crayons, cars going bad on cross-country trips, and attending undergraduate colleges in five states. In addition to his diagnosis of occupying time, he had a history of swimming in Lake Erie, hugging a Norwegian elkhound named Eric, sneaking out of screened windows on summer nights, loving men, teaching short story writing, and playing favorite uncle. In addition to his diagnosis of prostate cancer, he had a history of sailing past Point Loma where cerulean ceiling meets viridian floor. His last dose of study drug was 21 August 2006 and he reached primary efficacy endpoint in the study upon his terminus that day. His Serious Adverse Events were considered resolved on that date and assessed by the investigator as being related to being alive.

Gleason Score—a grading scale for prostate cancer, 5 + 5 indicating cells most cancer-like

He Sent Out Notice to the Rockiest Hills

Martin told his mother-in-law, Agnes that he had prostate cancer. But Agnes had lost many people she loved, including her husband, to cancer. Agnes said oh no three times, then interrupted Martin, pointed to the sky, and said, *Look at that jet! Look at its pure white contrail!*

Martin told his sister-in-law Sara that he had cancer. She checked his chakras with her jasper pendant, as if divining water. Then she passed her *Healing Hands* over his body several times, raking the coals of his life. *If you open your core, the energy can emanate*, her mantra repeated. Martin slept hard.

Martin told his brother-in-law, Jack that he had cancer. Jack said *Help me measure the depth of water below our dock*. Martin and Jack patiently plumbed the mudflats at high tide from a canoe, fathoming life below the surface. Ghost shrimp burrowed beneath them.

Martin told his brother Jon that he had cancer, but Jon had already died of prostate cancer two years earlier. Jon told Martin, *Lease with an option to buy*. As children, their games of Monopoly had lasted for days; the fight for *Boardwalk* and *Park Place*.

Martin told his brother Patrick that he had cancer. Patrick said I will re-determine my Gleason score, but I know I am at baseline.

Martin's wife Edith braised the beef, simmered the leeks, and vacuumed the floors. She boiled the potpourri Martin's mother June gave her a score of years ago before June had died of breast cancer.

Martin pondered baseline, lead line, plumb line, tagline, lifeline, bottom line. He pruned the grape vines in their yard, cut back the dead flax, and planted radish seeds. On Sunday he relaxed.

Pre-Op
    It is too bad for the space which finds itself a room

The walls in the tatami alcove filter light as Martin sits cross-legged on the floor. He watches the tissue paper between his spirit and his organs. The doctors make four holes in his core and thread vines into him. From the north comes an eye; from the west, a lasso; from the east, a laser; and the vine from the south carries several baggies. Martin watches his organs extrude through the holes in his body in zip-locked bags, leaving him cold. Soon, his organs appear in a kettle suspended over a small fire in the middle of the alcove.

Martin's mother June would sometimes take the body parts found inside a store-bought turkey—the neck, the liver, the gizzard, the kidneys—and boil them into a soothing broth. She drizzled beaten eggs into it and added green onions. Martin wants to ask his mother to send his Boy Scout bandana. He knows she saved it. He could use it to staunch the flow of organs. He wants to ask her how it felt to have strangers take her breast. He still remembers the zipper of puckered skin where her breast should have been. Her last night, nodules like mushroom caps sprouted from the roof of her mouth. He wants to ask her what she thinks of his children, both of them born since she died. But he will probably just ask for four Band-Aids. It might be easier and keep the conversation shorter. He is tired and she must be too.

Post-Op
> *I forgot to tell you, the risks are on the reverse side. Did you need to read them?*

The peristaltic pump clicks lactate ringers into Martin's gray face, puffing the sacks below his eyes. His slurred speech is not helped by ice chips dissolving his tongue's glue. When he can hold up his head, Martin counts the holes the robot has made in his abdomen; seven, the largest sideswiping his navel. One hole has a tube filling a small bottle with watery red. The others are sealed with transparent tape, the slits of eyes squeezed shut. Another tube carries deep green turning yellow from his bladder.

Martin carries his bags dutifully, drags them on the floor at night, tapes them to his leg by day. The histologist imbeds his organs in paraffin; slices them deli-style with a microtome. Cells, overcome by vacuoles, are tallied by the pathologist.

The surgeon says 80% chance of cure: one positive focal margin near the perineal invasion. Martin wonders which 20% of him will go. He watches the positive focal margin grow, extruding into nerves, conduits to his brain. His brain no longer conjugates the word *cancered*. Instead it differentiates the word. He examines his lesions each breakfast. At night he looks out from the cave of his head as he exhales. Night is darker than before.

Informed Consent
I cannot sleep, I get vertigo; yet I must face the enemy horizontally.

Martin's wife Edith reads aloud his directives. He has signed all the waivers and has released from liability the doctors, hospitals, wife, plant, animal, mineral, earth, air, fire, water, phthalates, PCBs, tectonic plates, and solar flares. Edith also reads aloud his hospital admission papers, confessing allergies to emotion, a religious preference to atheism, and his desired level of resurrection. Her soliloquy is accompanied by an orchestral "A" and unwavering line on his EEG. She closes the curtains in the hospital room and lets her lungs compress with his.

Martin lifts the ceiling. He walks onto the new dock at his brother-in-law's cabin, strides to the kayak tethered at the end of the float. He paddles into the fog surrounding Squaxin Island as his wife Edith lets out slack in the line. Somewhere to the southwest he knows Mt. Rainier's lenticular cap rides the troposphere like a beret. Martin pauses, his paddle balanced across the gunwale. Edith releases the line in a wave, the 3-prong plug on the floor.

Fresh Greyhound

Gross Description
It was a grapefruit. No really, a grapefruit the surgeons peeled from his peritoneal cavity. Pathologists didn't mention a rind or a smell. They did report colors ranging from yellow tan to tan to red. But they observed the mass was the size of a grapefruit and as such, it became a grapefruit to all who heard Eric's story.
Gross Description—Detail
Eric's grapefruit consisted of irregular clusters of atypical segments. It had incubated outside his stomach for an unknown length of time and went so far as to erode the dome of his bladder. His grapefruit had also grown a thin protuberance, searching for space to produce additional fruit. Lodged in the thoracic-4 vertebrae, the tentacle spiraled his spine from these until it cracked this cage, and it too, was peeled by the surgeon.
Thin Section Cytology
These aborted multimodal neoplasms of Eric's were precious grapefruit oddities. They were found to be decorated with goblets and signet rings, prized cells floating in pools of mucin. These rare finds were favored, pampered, stained, and preserved for possible immortalization.
Recommended Treatment
Eric hoped *Mucinex* would work, after the doctors named his grapefruit *mucinous cystic adenocarcinoma*; but instead, the names of various house-made cocktails were bandied about. Eric was 35 and moving in with his girlfriend next week.
Prognosis
Happy Hour is just beginning.

Fresh Greyhound: Cocktail consisting of 4 parts fresh grapefruit juice and 1 part gin or vodka, served over ice

Only I Get Vertigo

My hair is usually thin and gray, so I was surprised this morning to see it had turned into a mane of yellow ochre waves. My profile had become feline overnight, and I had a look of hirsute hauteur. This was particularly upsetting as I do not consider myself an arrogant person.

I made my way to the bus, worked my daily crossword puzzle, and walked from 3rd to 1st Avenue. I checked my reflection in the windows I passed and the storefront mirrors. Yes, I had the regal head of a lion, yet no one stared or gasped.

I found myself compelled to collect the carcasses of pigeons on my commute. Overnight there had been an unprecedented kill and they littered the sidewalks. Why should their lives be wasted? I'd eaten my usual breakfast of Cheerios at home so I carried them by neck or feet to The Market Tower, Floor 7. I pinned them to the burlap walls of my cubicle and waited for the muse. I felt confident she would visit today.

Graphis scripta

Code breakers, we all, and of treed
ancestors who still brachiate limb by limb

along the scribbles on the dark side of hardwoods.
Our alphabet withers like wasting starfish, arms gone missing,

hoping twisted caterpillars, conjoined 2 by 2, can bring
forth from the dark navels of their centromeres

cairn-shaped inuksuks, showing a path
where the underbrush of nurture has not.

These are lichens letting us know, like an ultrasound,
what might lie ahead, the writing on the wall showing that

a translocation, a shifted limb or finger, a word or line
break moved here or there could change the meaning

of life as we know it. And if the chromosomal squash shows only a partial
of 23 pairs, does this become somebody else's problem or merely

somebody else's poem.

Graphis scripta—script lichen

The Stronger Bond

Seventh grade, in search of a science project,
I am watching my father explain the pulping process,
how much stronger the beta bond than the alpha
between glucose units in cellulose versus starch.
His fingers assume molecular conformations.
His hands gesticulate the expulsion of water.
The polymer lengthens under his tutelage leaving
an oxygen between each ring. There is rapture
in his face, fervor in his voice. His eyes
see bonds forming, breaking, re-forming
as hybrid orbitals overlap, as atoms
share electrons once again.

Magrob

Collage of leaves and plump red lured me to the tree
I did not see as mirrored. Swooping for the snatch,
I came to rest mid-beat against the scene,
my final act, a Rorschach of spread wings against the glass.

Upon cement, my body paid no heed to me nor did my feet—
my beak mouthed mute a trill, the only sound—the shrill of flies
I did not feel until they sipped the fluids from my eyes
and laid their spawn in flesh against my will.

But now I am become Magrob, robin changed by maggots
as my body, robbed of warmth, begins to cool toward heaven.
My entrails squirm, cleaned by their larvae. Gangrene melts,
and now I spread the word. To be reborn means to embrace what rots.

Travel with me Ormalot, I am cold

Ormalot extends her hands
toward the carcass, warming them,
inhaling the exothermic.
Plants won't do for her—
their carbon locked inextricably.
Only decaying flesh provides
the entropy she craves.

Ormalot searches the pits of new construction,
examines the spoor of back hoes,
scours fresh landslides. At each excavation
she paws the potsherds and middens,
grazing for the irreversible loss.
If need be, she'll camp over landfills,
blow out the methane flares and suck
the slurry of gases venting
through chimneys like straws.

In backyards she can sense the energy seep
beneath the stone placed over the not-yet-bare
bones of a tabby, the remnants
glowing with barely perceptible heat,
polypeptides unraveling.

She hates graveyards. Liners protect the boxes;
boxes protect the bodies; the bodies sleep preserved.
Decomposition so slow, Ormalot's toes get frostbite.
Metacarpals of her first two fingers have fused
forming the prying half of a hammer head
She wants to wander the field of chiseled stones,
pry open the lids one by one, let oxygen do its work,
breaking the bonds, releasing the heat,
warm herself in the quieting chaos.

The Strings

The conductor keeps his eyes downcast, his
supraorbital tori bleed shadows. He listens
with enlarged bivalves hinged to his head
to the immutable roar. He takes her to a place
where horsetails snake between the legs
of buttresses propping up Notre Dame,
between the Eiffel girders supporting no electricity.
He takes her where avian guano erodes cornices
and ices the gargoyles. He coos. They coo.
They more than coo.

The planes drone the loss
of earth, the rarefied air. A hooded
figure on the taxi-way waves, gloved
hand cupped, arm in a sickle swath of harvest,
air rushing to fill the void behind his sweep.

The conductor hushes her, caresses her
lips with the back of his fingers, pinches her lips
between finger and thumb, covers her
scream with his palm, the sun a wan
ball at the end of the runway.

Refractory
for my parents

They realized later they should have known what
the doctor would tell them when the receptionist checked
them in without looking up.

How annual colonoscopies for five years
hadn't found metastasis until now,
constriction forcing biopsy through colon walls.

Scan results confirmed the spread.
Prostate, bladder, liver—both lobes,
shadows on every piece of film.

The receptionist was not at her desk as they put
one foot in front of the other and found their car,
drove in silence four miles out Webb Hill Road.

Where clear-cuts gave full view of the Olympics,
they pulled off, held each other,
tried out the word, *Terminal*.
Like a destination.

The Sun's Rake

That autumnal walk lingers, the way
smells do for most people. We edged
the power lines, their shadows like hurdles in our path.
When I was little you told me we could walk
this route to the ocean and never cross a road.

We were stopped by construction at an open pit,
the highway bypass cut to preserve
our small town center. I asked point blank,
Do you believe in a life hereafter?

It wouldn't be fair otherwise seemed a strange answer
from a man who viewed his cancer as a statistic.
I wasn't used to scientists talking fairness.
I wasn't used to you talking death.

The Sunday before Father's Day, we stood
in a semicircle around your bed, releasing your body, the eastern
curtains open to filtered rays of dawn. We just assumed
we would feel your presence ever after.

I asked Mom only once, months later,
Do you ever feel that Dad is near you?
Her face fell as she admitted,
she too, remains in the dark.

After 911

After they finally let me into the ER past midnight
while sines and cosines mingled on monitors,
pulse in red, breath in blue,
After they'd stopped
your heart, (the paddle burn, a red
outline on your chest for weeks),
After your cardiomyocytes began to beat in unison again
I wish I'd said to you just once, *I love you,*
Before you became conscious of fluorescent
lights, pills, the ride home, sleep,
and work the next day.

Interdigitating Phalanges

Rooted in wrist, branching to tips, blue on the outside, red
beneath. They reach for raised dots with nearly
more neurons per square millimeter than
any other part of the body. Crescent lunula rise
on their backs behind keratin
curtains and cuticle nurture. Soft
underbellies splay arches, whorls, ridges, loops,
bifurcations, islands, spirals, accidentals.
The five of them, woof and warp to yet
another five, share collagen and oils without
protection. Smiles on knuckles
deepen. To hold is to have.

Power Lines

A neon greyhound runs the power lines.
Each crevice in the siding of the station
houses a pigeon, a thin white message
wrapped around one leg.

The pay phone doesn't work.
There are no quarters in the coin return.
The parking meter flies a red flag.
You can't see your reflection in the store windows.
You left here yesterday. You left here a score of years ago.
You know you never left.
A movement at the second story window tells you so.

Those men pinned to benches in ennui
lost themselves the year they never found the body
of the lad who drowned in Goldsborough Creek.
For days they searched the mudflats at low tide.
They still do, confessing to ghost shrimp.

One of them was the boy who couldn't turn-in his
friend, stuck in the furnace vent at *Johnny's Music Box*,
the two of them filching sheet music.
His friend's body, discovered days later by the storeroom stench,
salmon rotting on the beach.

Coca cola in red italics cannot dilute the salt.
Stones echo heat and the barbershop pole won't spin.
You roam the warm cement at night searching
for coins to pay the meter, or make the call,
the pigeon's message lost.

Daphne odora

Paula, you forced
their constellations
in January, the heady
fragrance of jasmine turning
us into fools.

If only
you could have transformed
yourself, escaping tumor
after tumor.

Susan E. Hamilton, a native of western Washington, has spent more than the last decade writing up clinical study data for biotech companies in the therapeutic areas of respiratory diseases, inflammation, and oncology. The plight of the patients she has described, both in study reports and in poetry have affected her personally. Prior to medical writing, she did pharmacological research on muscarinic receptors in the brain, signal-transduction research on retinal cells, and oceanographic research measuring organic compounds in sediments and the water column.

Her works have appeared in Pacific Northwest publications including *Floating Bridge Review, Switched-on Gutenberg, Magnolia News/Queen Anne News, Arnazella, Beyond Parallax, Between the Lines, Signals, West Wind Review, The Written Arts, The Duckabush Journal, Spindrift,* and *Poetry Seattle.*

www.ingramcontent.com/pod-product-compliance
Lightning Source LLC
LaVergne TN
LVHW041523070426
835507LV00012B/1789